Go ahead
I'm listening.

By

Bliss August

BookLeaf
Publishing

India | USA | UK

Presentation by *BookLeaf Publishing*

Web: www.bookleafpub.com

E-mail: info@bookleafpub.com

ISBN: 9789357443258

First edition 2022

DEDICATION

To my mother,

Because, above all, she believed in me the most.

ACKNOWLEDGEMENTS

I would not know where to start.

To all of those at Bookleaf Publishing for allowing me this excellent opportunity to turn my private thoughts into public sharing.

To, LJ* for confiding in me and growing up alongside me.

To, AW* for putting up with and tolerating me through this journey (and for putting Maggie to bed so I could finish all the multiple patient notes, exam marking and moreover this book!)

To ZV* for the endless conversations and gentle encouraging nudges.

To my mummy village. For being the best bunch of cheerleaders any woman and mother could ask for. You know who you are!

And to T for everything else.

*abbreviated to protect the innocent.

PREFACE

First thing I had to do was Google 'What is a preface to a book?'

To me, a preface is the face I wake up with in the morning before I do a paint job which will turn out to be my 'real face' when mummying or at work. But I'm guessing I would not sell many books if there was photo of my 'pre face' on it.

Now understanding, after copious amounts of scrolling through examples on the internet, it is an explanation of why I wrote this book of poems and why you should read it.

Well, everyone goes through tough times and everyone has differing ways of dealing with it. Disgruntled patients, rows with loved ones, failing assignments or struggling to entertain your toddler on an English rainy day, one cannot help but be human about the whole thing.

My way of letting go and being human was to write short poems, leaving behind the therapist, the lecturer, the mother and just being Bliss.

I hope, above all else, you realise too that your own therapists, your professors, your teachers, your fellow mummies are all human first and the other stuff second.

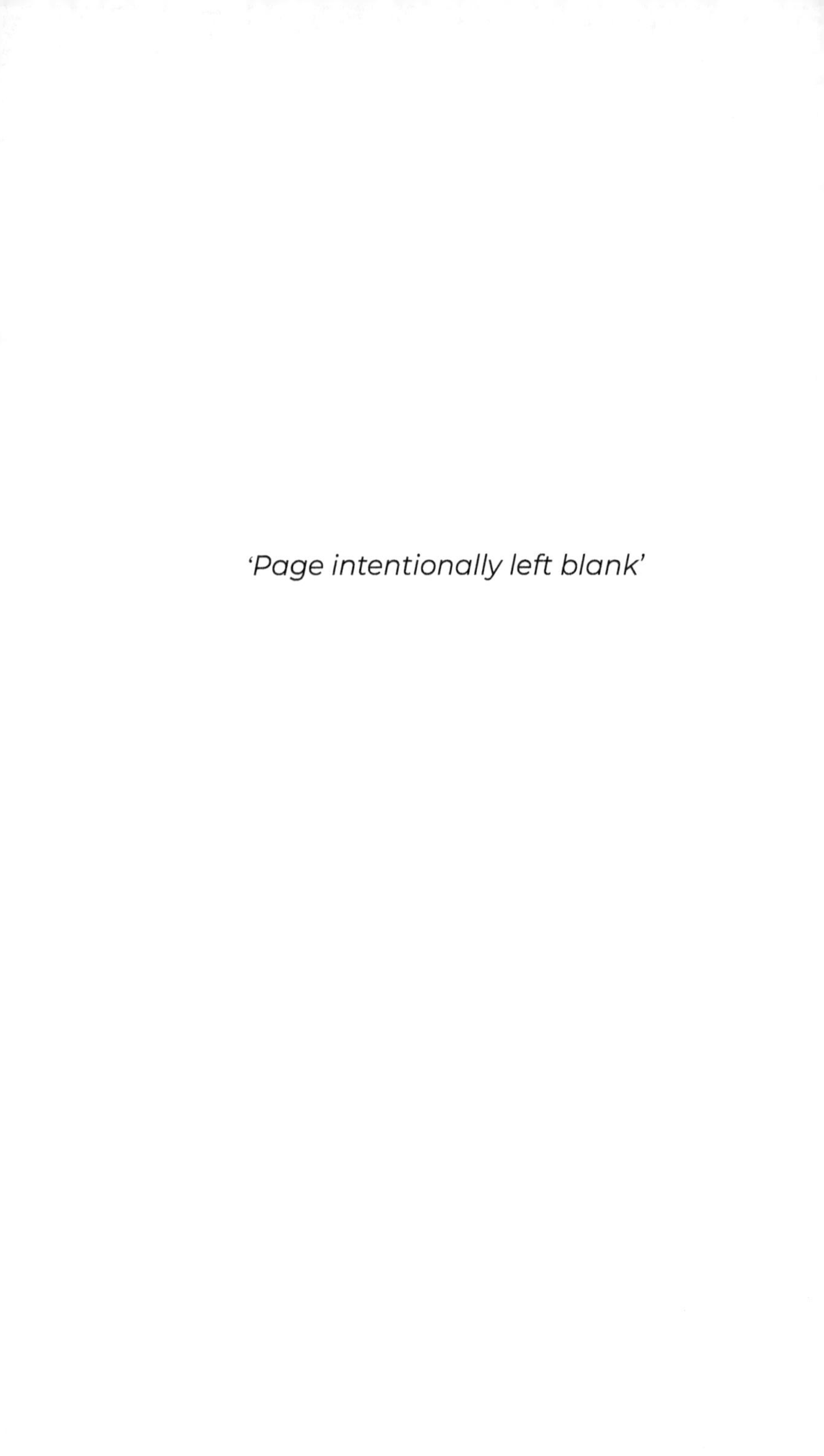

'Page intentionally left blank'

The very thing for kisses, Bliss is.

My baby, has a mottled fisk.
My baby has a neck in creases,
My baby kisses and is kissed
For she's the very thing for kisses,
Bliss is.

Written by Bliss' mother (August 1987)

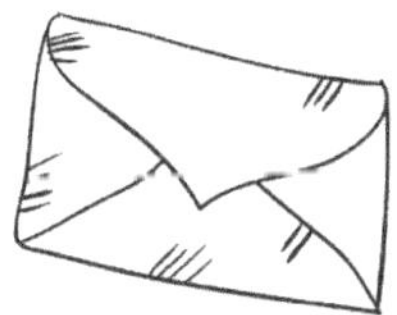

Bliss' reply to mother.

To love is a skill shown within home.
Taught, closeness and intimacy are
welcome.
Passed on through legacy,
Planted within me and grown
alongside my veins.
I now love boldly, bravely and wholly
As a result of your kisses,
this is.

Reply written October 2021

Siblings Unite
in their Kingdom

I'm gay – he said.
I know – she acknowledged.
You do? – he replied
We've grown up together- she
remarked
Does it change things? – he asked
Not in the slightest – she assured

Shall we talk to mum? – he wondered
What do **you** want to do? – she
enquired
I just want to sit a while – he suggested

After a while

I didn't choose this. – he uttered

You're choosing to be yourself and
that's the most beautiful – she ended.

Magpies are bastards.

One for sorrow
Two for joy
Do you know how many times I see
one
Just one.

Because of some involuntary
hereditary of superstition
I desperately do all the things one
'should' do
When faced with the above situation.
Of only seeing one magpie.

Shout: WHERE'S YOUR FRIEND?
Hoping it may reply or even more
helpful, point.
Desperately seeking another
to turn the despair into a triumph

Say: Hello Mister Magpie how's your
sons and daughters?
Do they even know which are their
sons and which are their daughters?
And actually how does this help?

Salute: Raise one hand to your head -
even if driving!

Hold: your collar until you see a four
legged animal
Please don't ask me about this one.

After failing the above,
brace yourself to be swallowed by
sorrow
And then when something
negative happens in your day
Blame the magpie,
That silly magpie.

Magpies are bastards.

The ride.

From the ground,
Fire ready to burn
One hell of a rocket ride prepares
For stargazing voyage

Cookie cutter roles
Not for me
I aim high
Proving my worth
Waiting for the words
'We are proud of you'.

The fire capable of burning others
Without realising
An overshadow with no malice
A spotlight with no space.

It's a selfish journey
A one woman show
A single ticket
To perfectionism.

Replaced

You broke me into easier pieces to chew,
You also turned my insides into something
new.
My heart might be sellotaped
But my soul is glowing
I hated you for a time
And my fear is that it's showing

But I now look at the woman in the mirror
And see behind her shine
Now someone else falls under fairy lights
And their face has replaced mine.

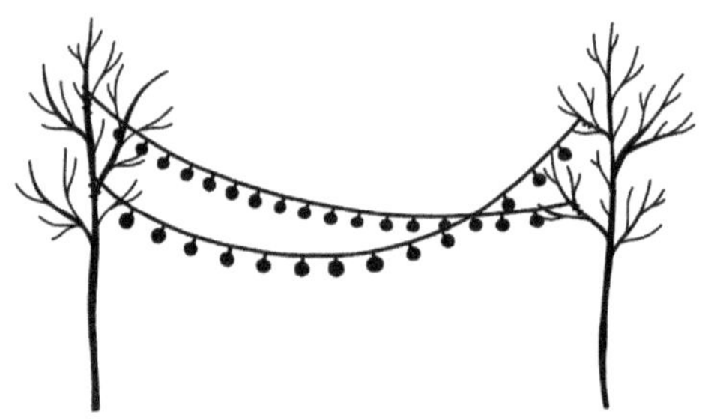

The day you left.

You just left.
You cut the cord
No advance warning
You didn't glance back
To see tears rolling

Too young to understand
But too old to ignore
I forgave you otherwise
It was us versus us
Time and time again.

Our blood was not thick enough
If you must kill us
Then please tell us why.

You've missed out on the girl
who now wears women's clothing.
She is pure and she does good
What a pity that you are the very
bones of her
Yet your name is no longer engraved.

The book we write.

Innocent and hopeful beginning,
Narrative about to unfold,
With every passing chapter
A story starting to be told.

Yes! There was a plot twist
A period of absence
Multiple drama and happenings
A marriage of accidental meeting.

The pages were not the same
The characters had altered
The fairy tale, now textbook
Still remains unfinished.

Place it back on the shelf,
Hide it in some loft.
Read it from time to time and wonder
If it's ever time to write again.

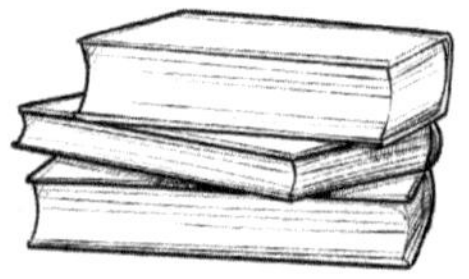

When in doubt,
add water .

Bathe in a bubble bath,
Water the plants,
Add some to paint to create,
Sip a drink,
Swim in a pool,
Dance in the rain,
Jump in the puddle,

and above all - cry.

It's ok.

The Unlikely Friendship

An unexpected surprise
Of uncertain meeting
Unrelated agendas yet
Union in converse
Unlike any other

Until now
Unsure of paths
United in interview, oh
Unassuming man

Unfortunate of distance however
Unnerved by truth
Unique fullness
Of the unlikely friendship.

To all my clients.

I'm no good with goodbyes,
which in my job is a curse

I hope you are well
know that I think of you

We always finish the same,
saying...
in the nicest possible way
we hope to never meet again.

Talking of ends, at the beginning
Undesirably becoming a habit in life
For who talks of the finish line at the
start?
If only to make the freedom more fair.

Lost

I am the deaf and the dumb
No fit in space,
I have no place,
No music can erase.

For I gave it up
to seek adventure
which did not measure
No move left to make.

I smell smoke from flames
closest to hell one's been
toes feel its warmth

My wings will take flight
To greener grass of old
To belong once more
and begin again.

Prefer loving you from a distance

In all these years, months, weeks and
hours
That we have spent in close proximity
The living, the working, the socialising
I fear my patience is now empty

I no longer crave your attention or
affection
I no longer need my mate
For all the things I liked about you
Have transformed to things I hate

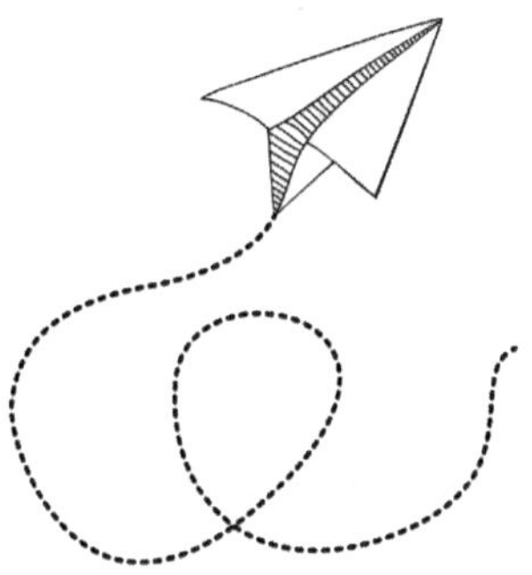

She called him a knob.

Now listen,
I am no snob, I've been brought up
well
to say good morning , to kiss good
tonight
to say this evenings been swell

Driving with mum
the queen of elegance
Not a hair out of place
Nothing but smiles on face

We drive in the car to songs before I
was born
We don't just sing on the road, we
perform!

However, there's one thing that
happens
When we are out hitting the open way
this exquisite elegance
turns into commonness peasants
and she comments on others passing
by.

Now listen to me
I am no snob
but I'll never forget the time

My mum called another driver a knob!

Dare you to set sins free

Dare you to set sins free,
hurt had its holding,
push away darkness
that covered once was light.

A man with heart too full,
words a plenty,
brain too wondrous,
speaks so ill of past
is still just a man.

No shame in seeking
beauty.
For we too are just men,
And prison held in mind.

Hands and hearts

Hand taken by one,
a heart another
eyes that clearly see
to the soul,

Am I torn or tied?
As my chest
continues to ache.

Drain dry as it longs for more,
more than what can be offered before.
Words or promises that feel empty
now.
Moon passes by night, by day
Feelings are not fading away.

Are the words new?
Or are they offered to a few?
for no reason or will it be a season?
Hunger, my desire, my need
To belong to you
Be confused by you
Be consumed by you
I want you.

Trembling.

Trembling
At your finger,
I'm lifted

Out of carnal
into sweet hereafter
You didn't just look
You saw.

Moss frame diminished
Art naked bare

Venus, on some high.
You knelt;
In worship.

A religion
We cannot breathe .

Intoxicating; inviting
Alluring; arousal.

Press against me
Let's share this vibrant way.

Neither body ashamed
But together in time.

Restoring femininity
Never desired you more.

Touch me again
Trembling

At your finger.

You are dad.

Our genes don't match
but our hearts sure do.

My ego was bruised
And without words
You soothed it.

You stepped up to the plate
another man left on the table

For that I am grateful, always.
To me.

You are dad.

To his future her.

Let him space
To not lose face
Let him time
To avoid decline
Let him know
That he is cared for so
Let him keep
When the journey's steep

Let him stay
Through multiple Mays
Let him wander
For the battle yonder
Let him push
To the edge of Hindu Kush
Let him gaze
At setting sun rays

Let him forget
Under no threat
Let him success
No pawns in chess
Let him mistakes
No matter the quakes it shakes

Let him sing
Sit patiently on wing

Let him believe
No tricks up sleeve
Let him tea
With a view to see
Let him togetherness
No competition of cleverness

Let him truth
In age and youth

Let him live.

Love Letter

Hey you,

Meeting you was like knowing you were going to be a song I played on repeat.

I am the happiest woman since I found you and I will do I can to keep you this way and make sure you feel appreciated.

I want to spoil you, encourage you and be that gentle breeze that blows the bad feelings away.

I know you are not perfect, I do not want you to be.
You are a part of me and belong to me.

You are important to me and I will do what I can to keep your dream in tact and on track.

Bliss, you are loved.

And most importantly deserve to love yourself a little more.

Kindest regards

Me.

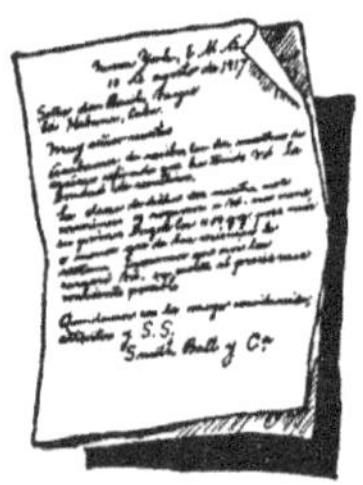

What is it baby?

As she enthusiastically scribbles,
Not deciding, just drawing.
Now taking the same advice in my life.

Not sure what I'm making,
Just creating my way through.

Will decide what it is later on
Like this poem actually...
I didn't know where it was going
And here we are.

You ended up here at the end
With me.

Thanks baby
you teach me more about living every
day

No need to know the end result

Just be enthusiastic about scribbling
along the way.

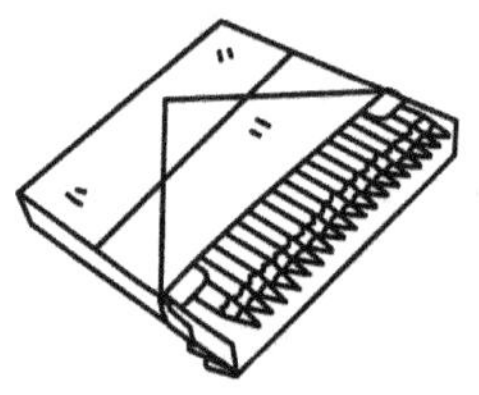